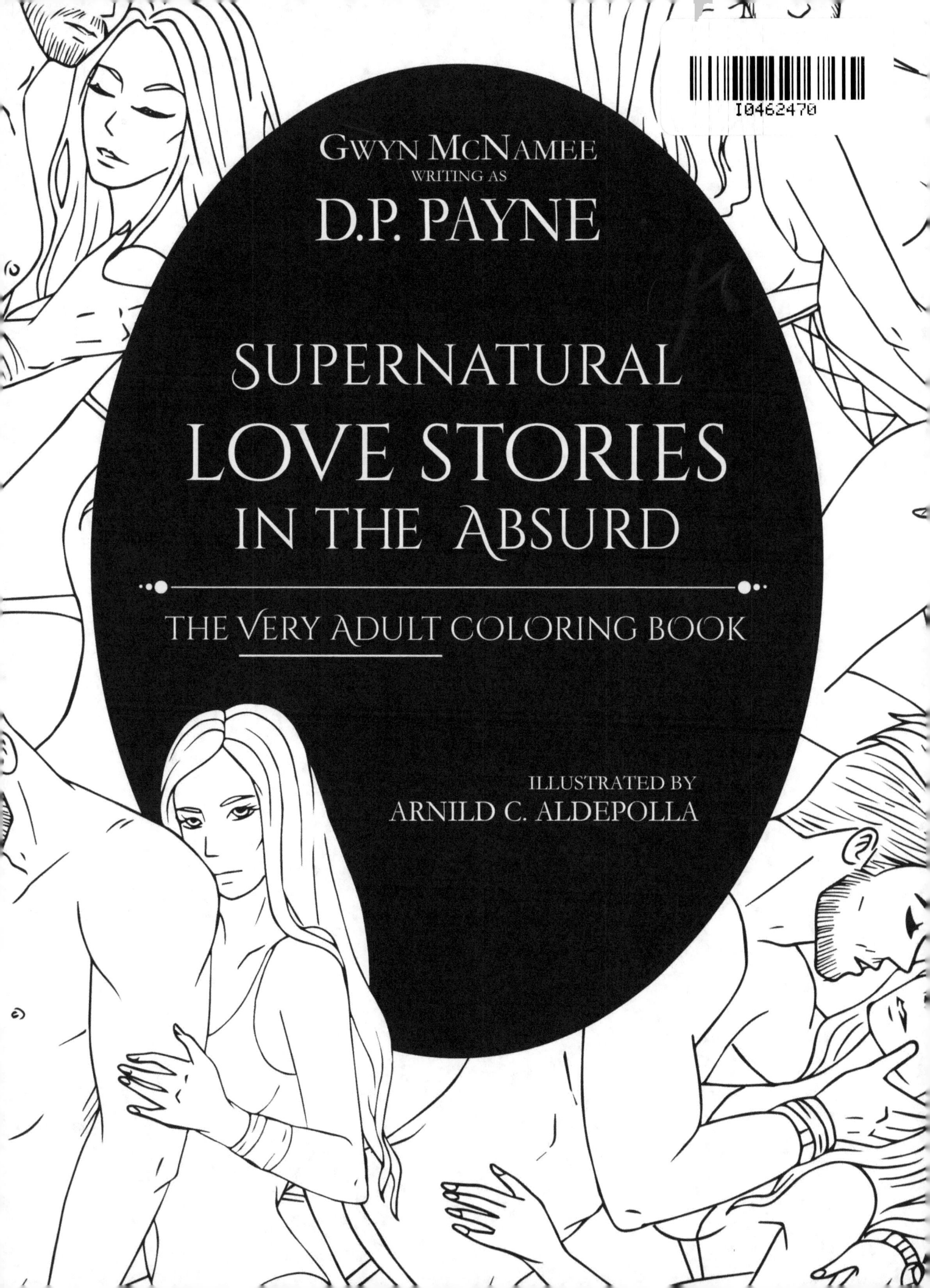

GWYN MCNAMEE
WRITING AS
D.P. PAYNE

SUPERNATURAL
LOVE STORIES
IN THE ABSURD

THE VERY ADULT COLORING BOOK

ILLUSTRATED BY
ARNILD C. ALDEPOLLA

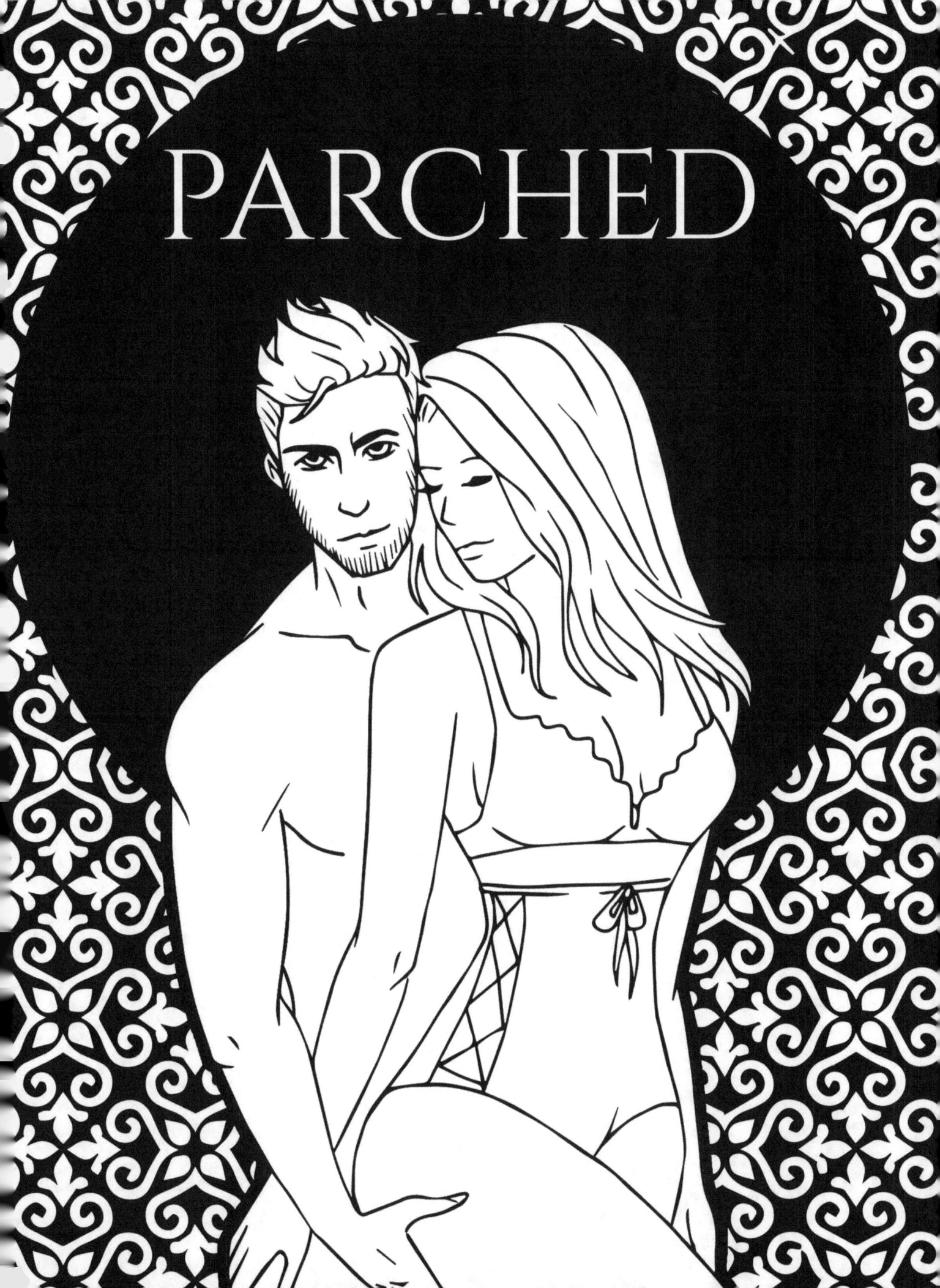

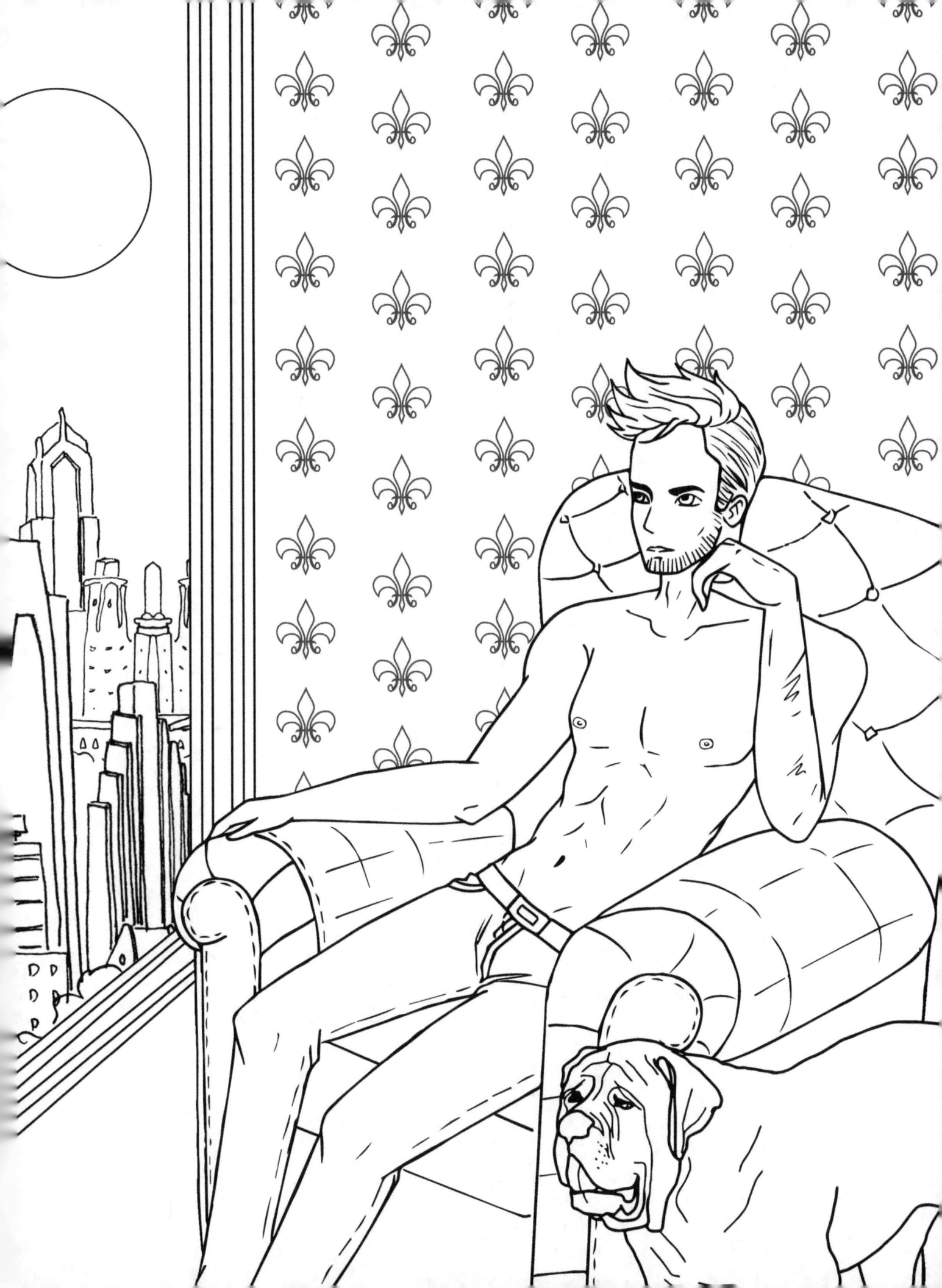

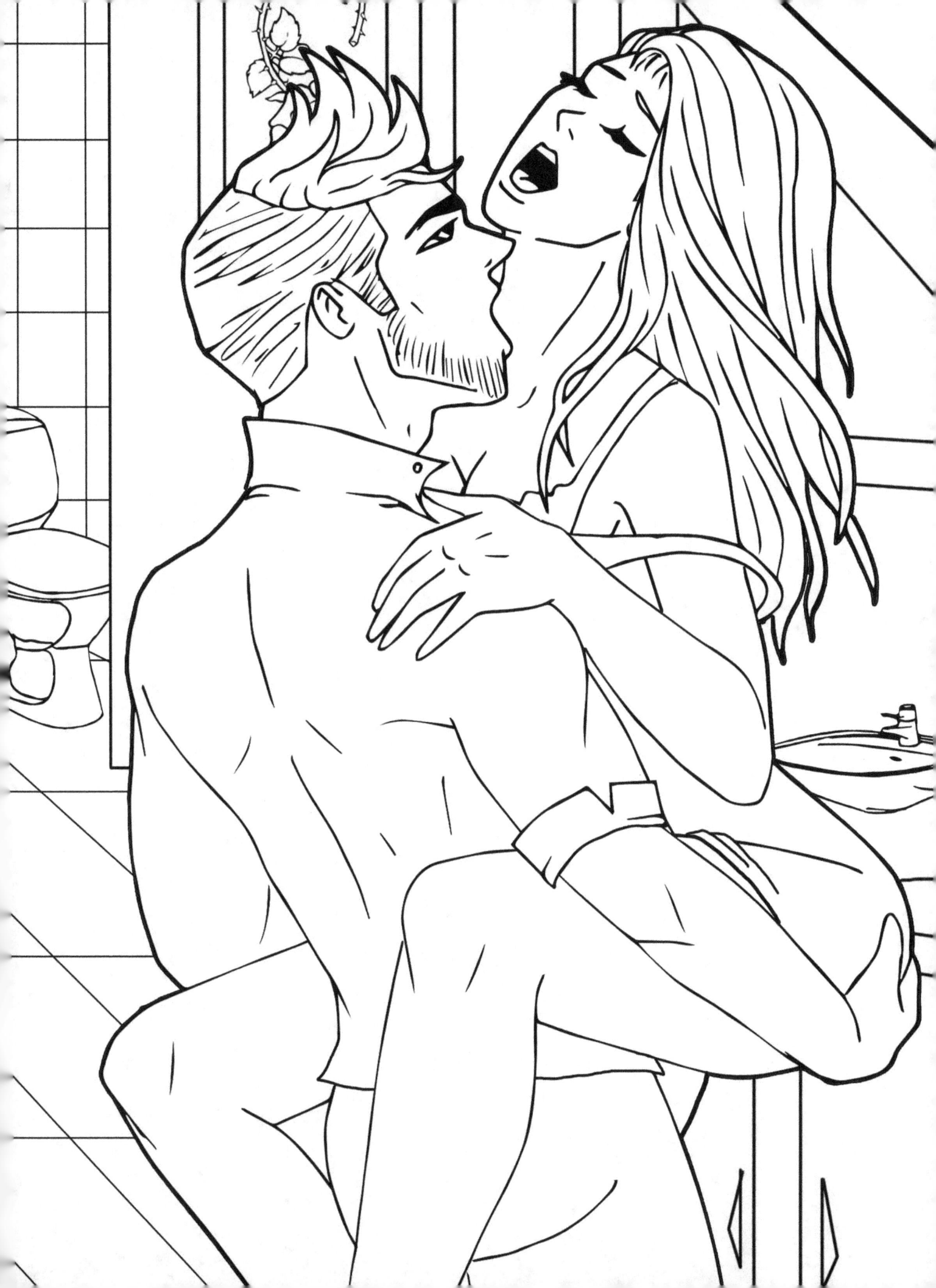

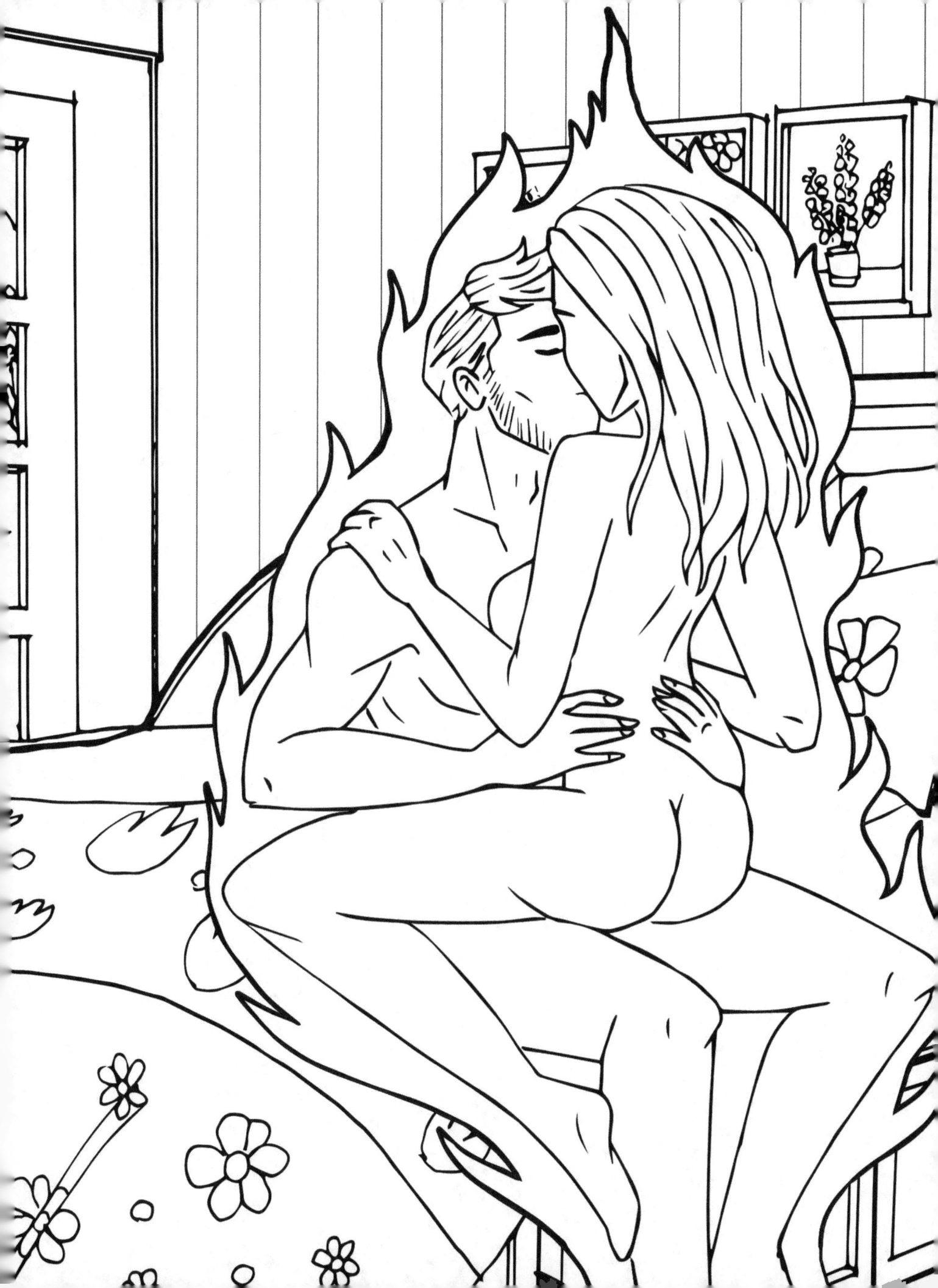

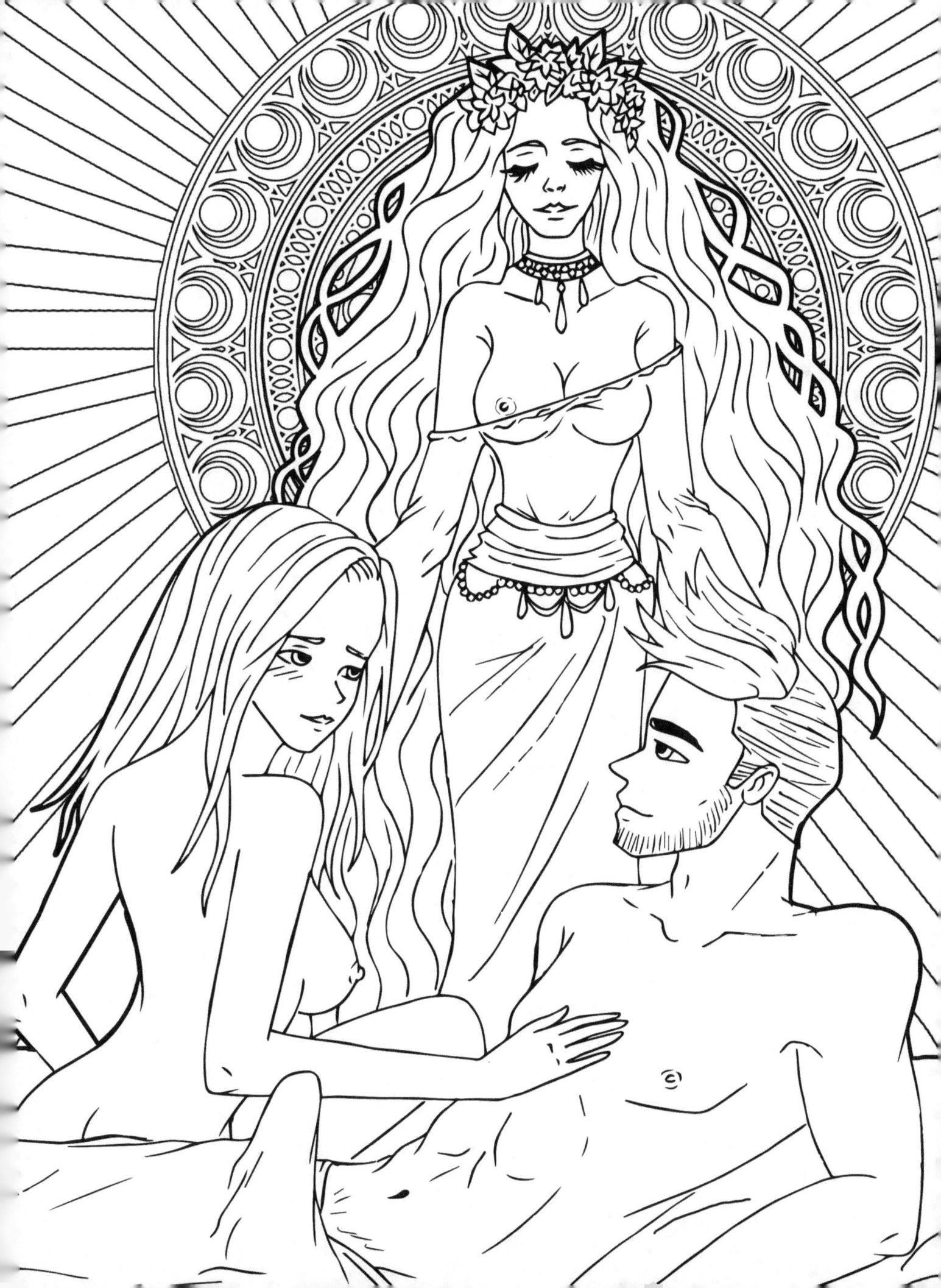

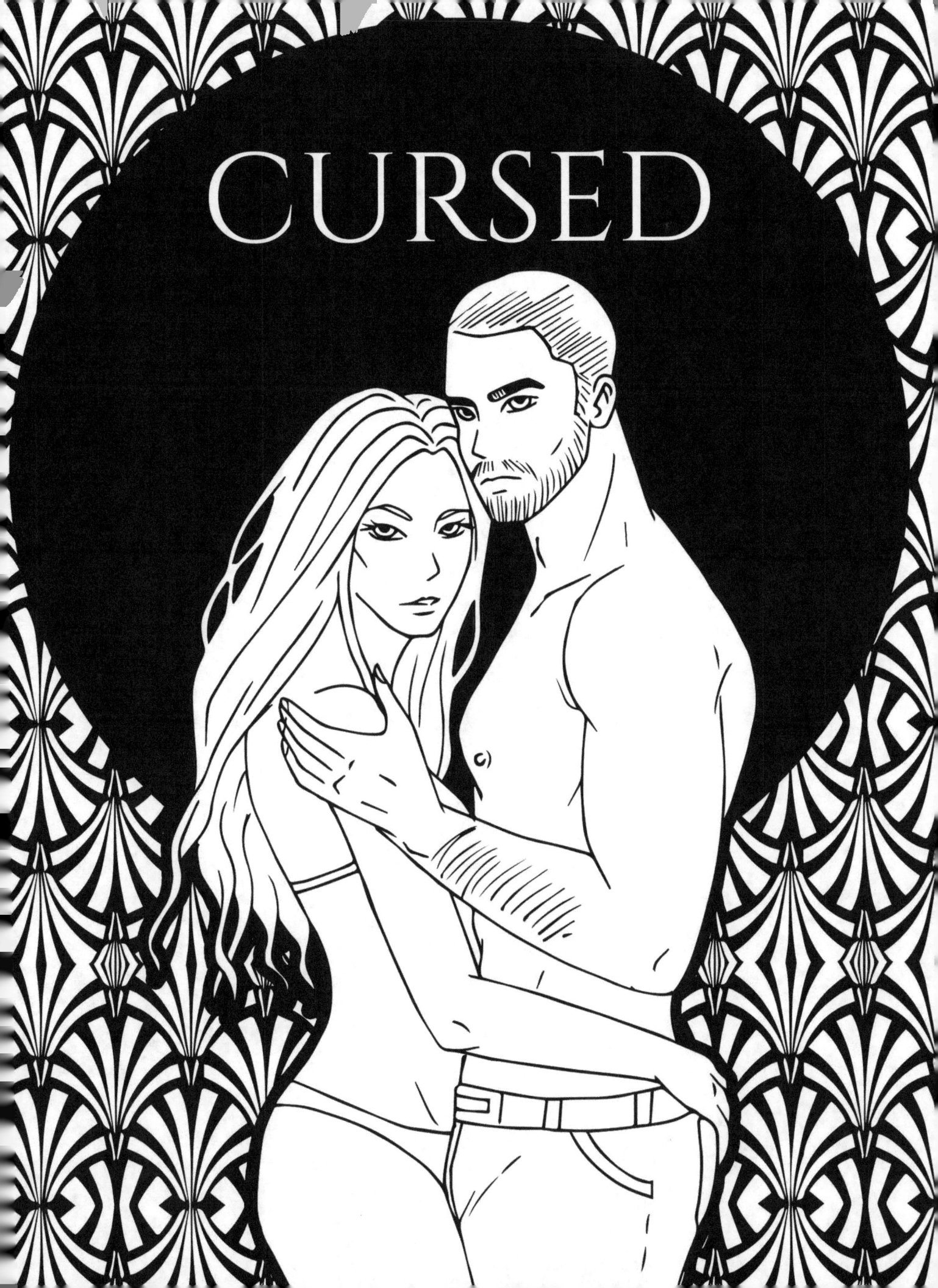

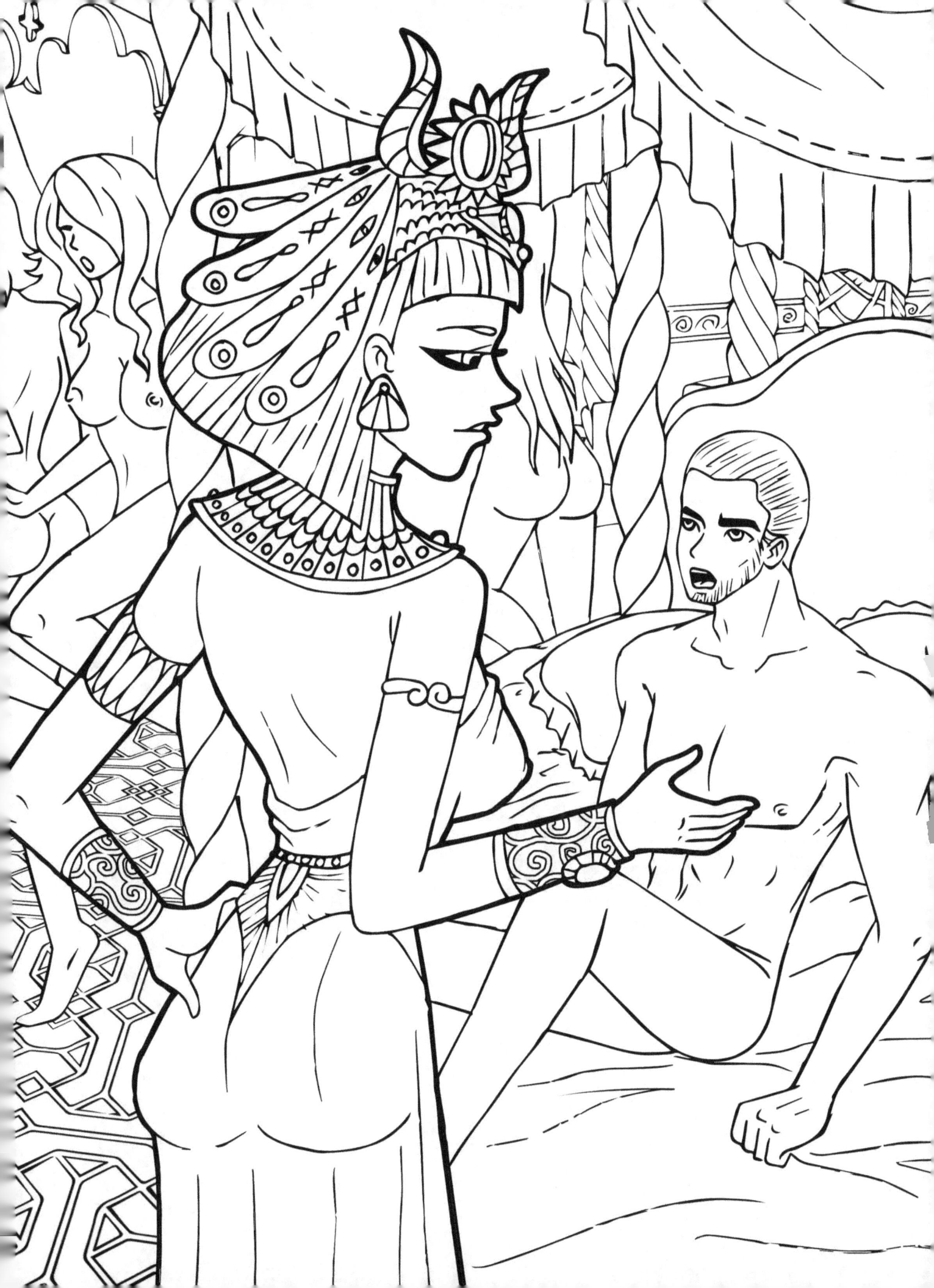

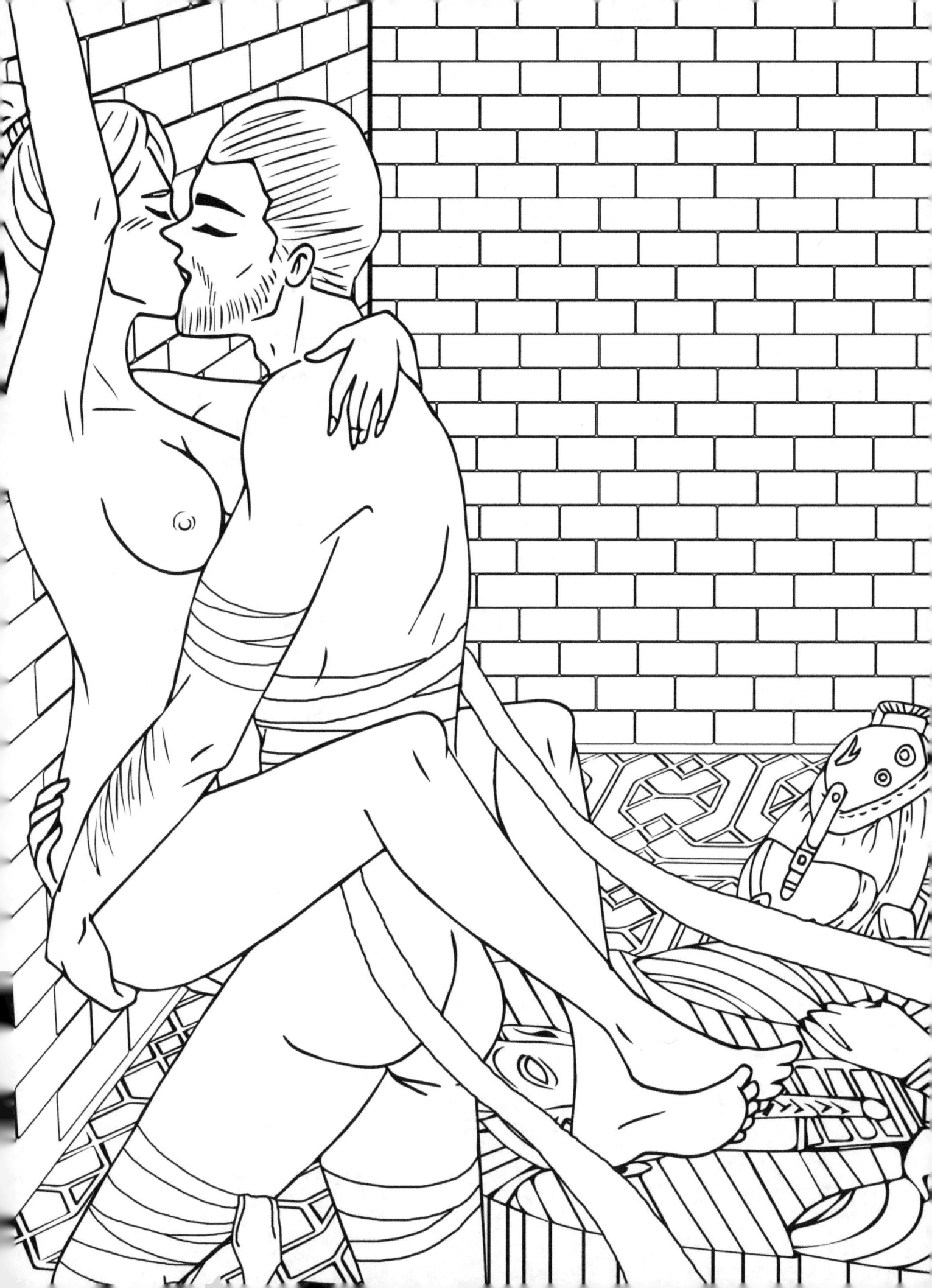

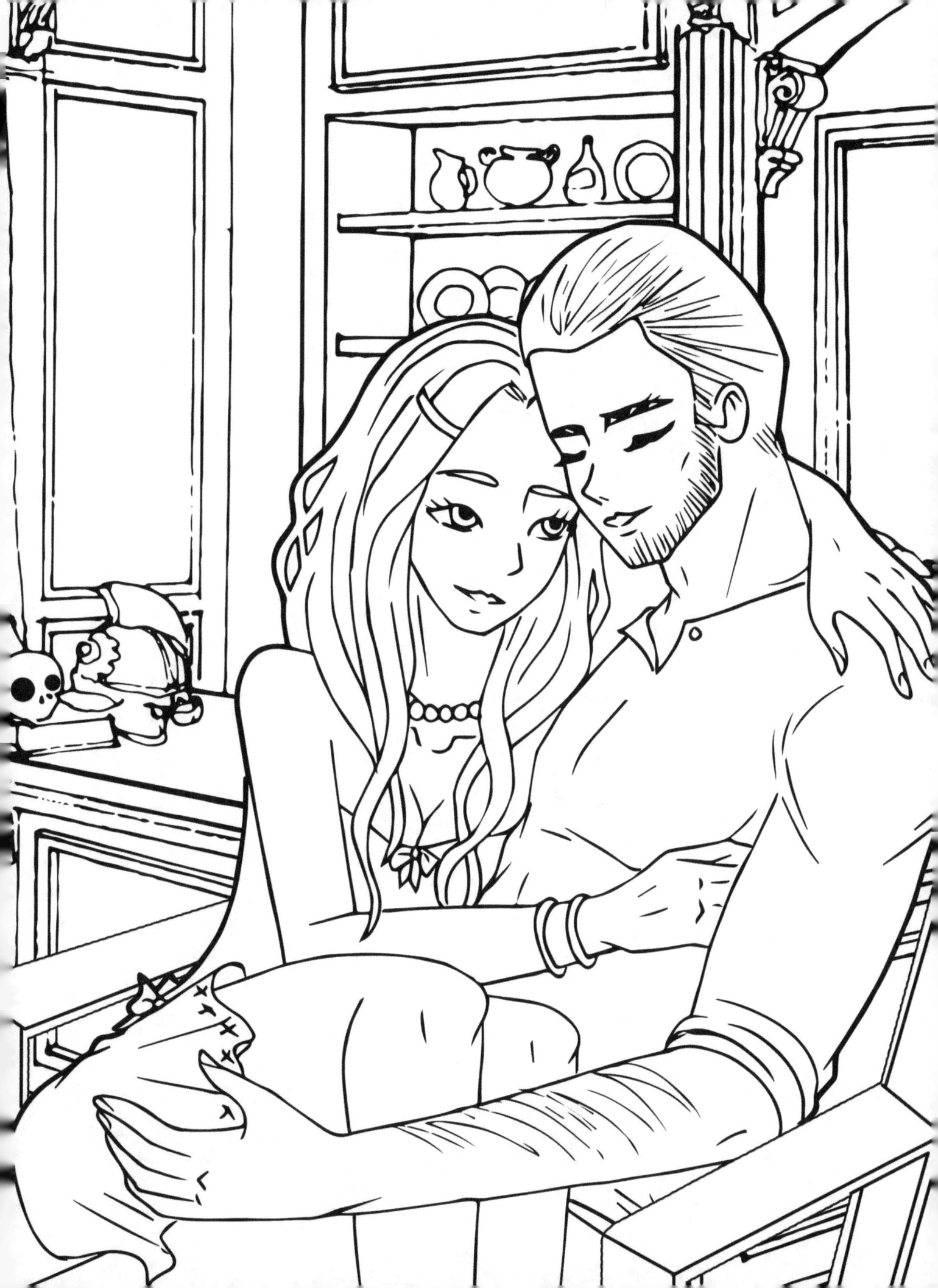

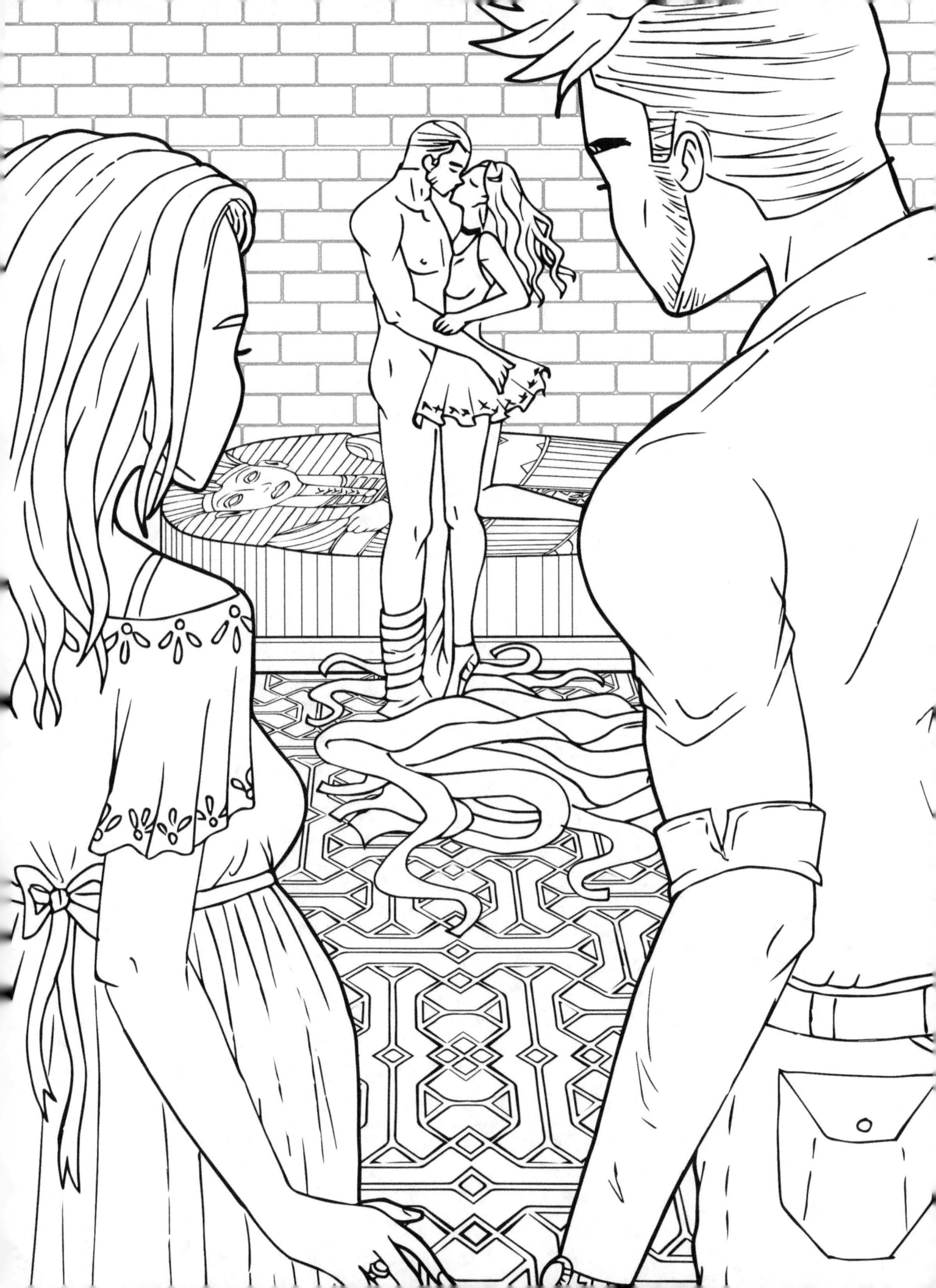

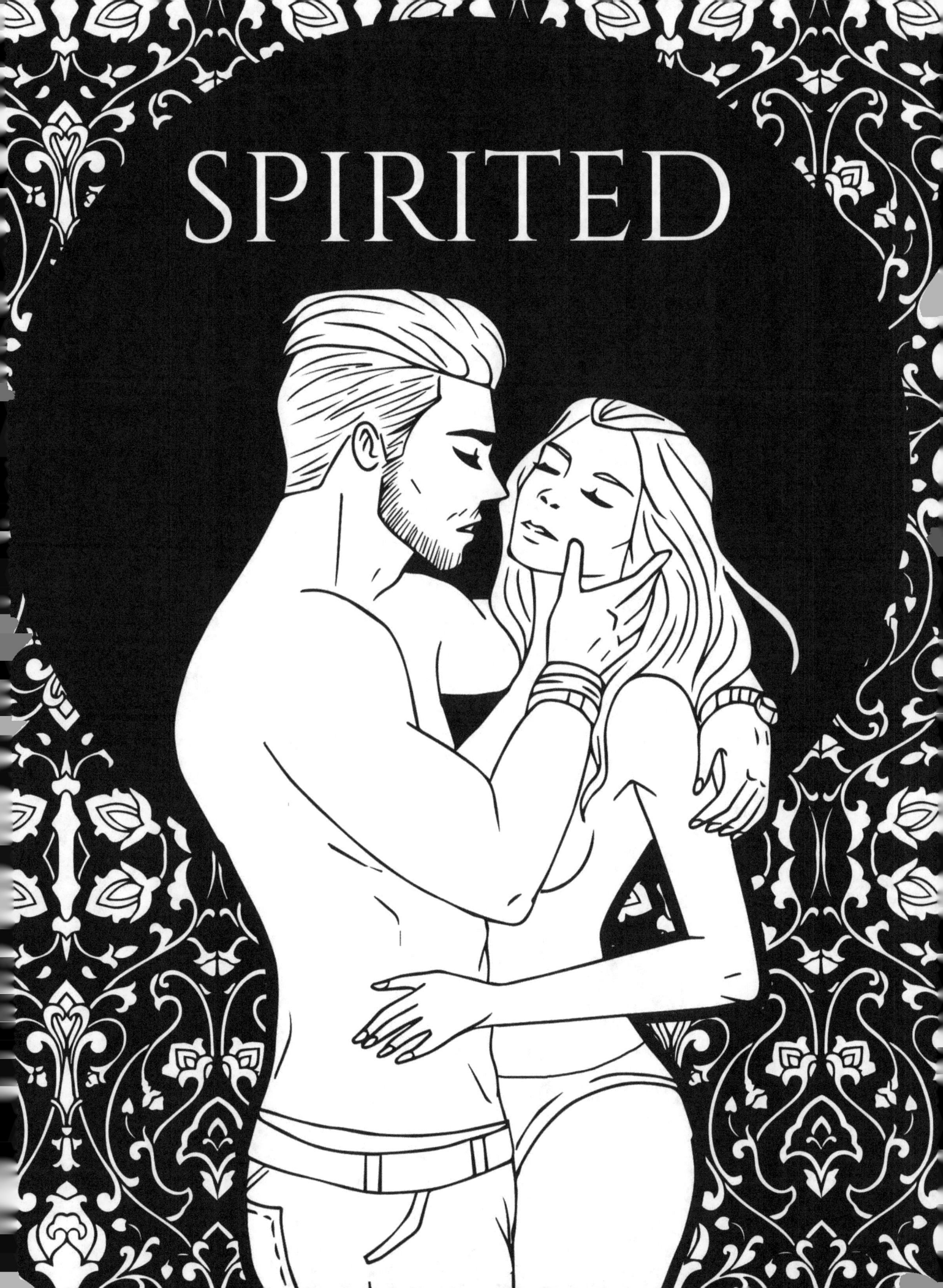

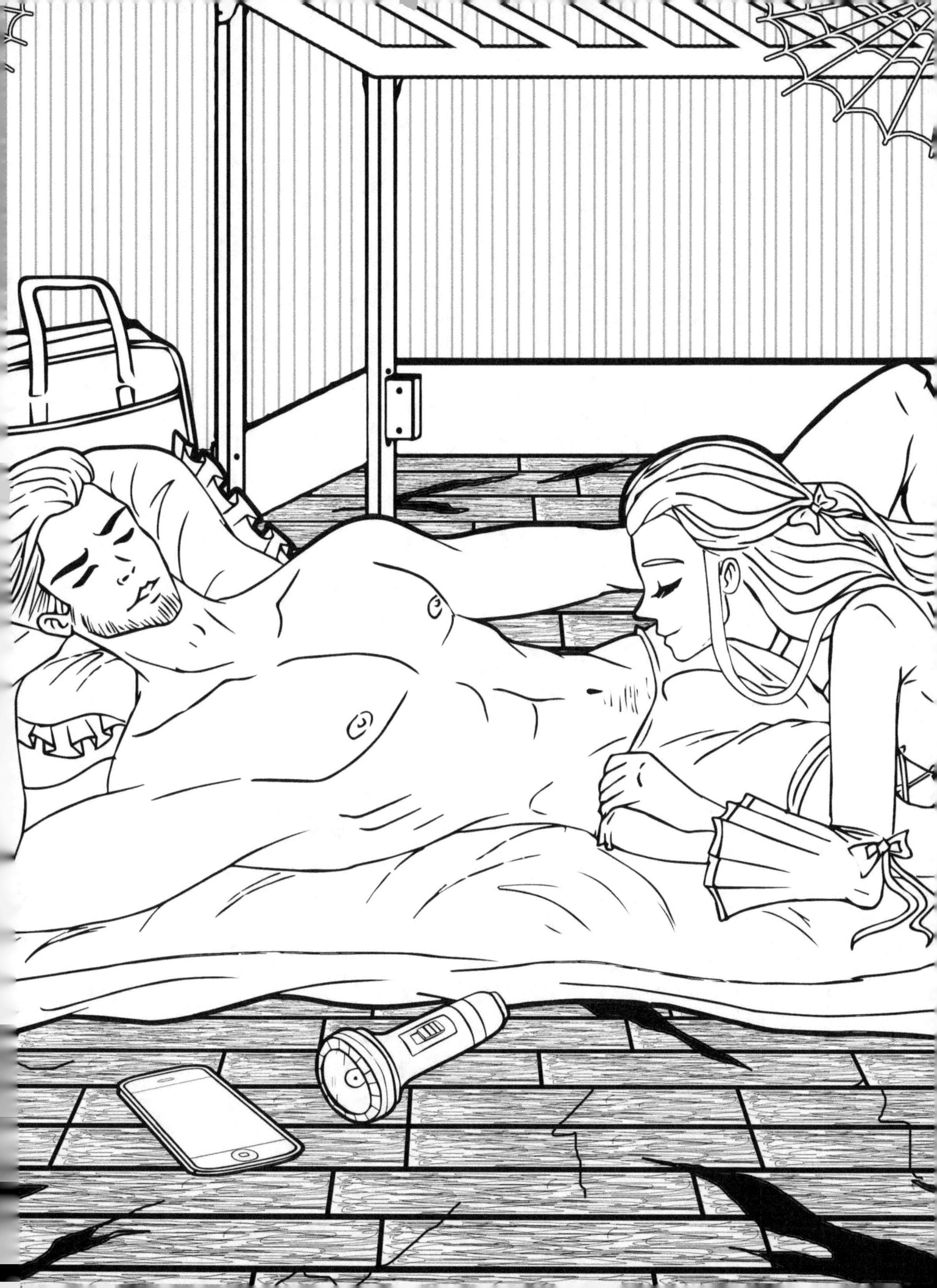

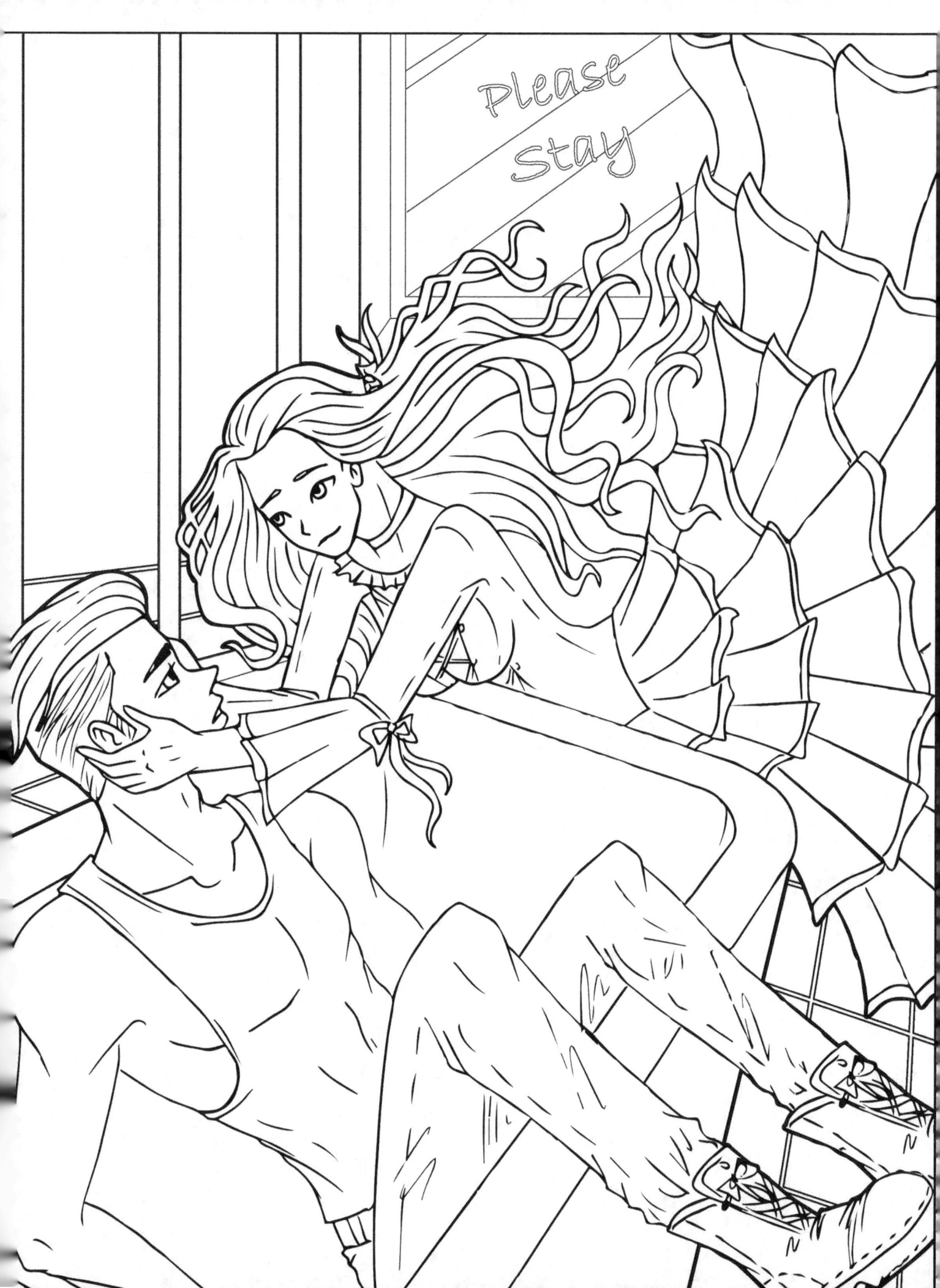

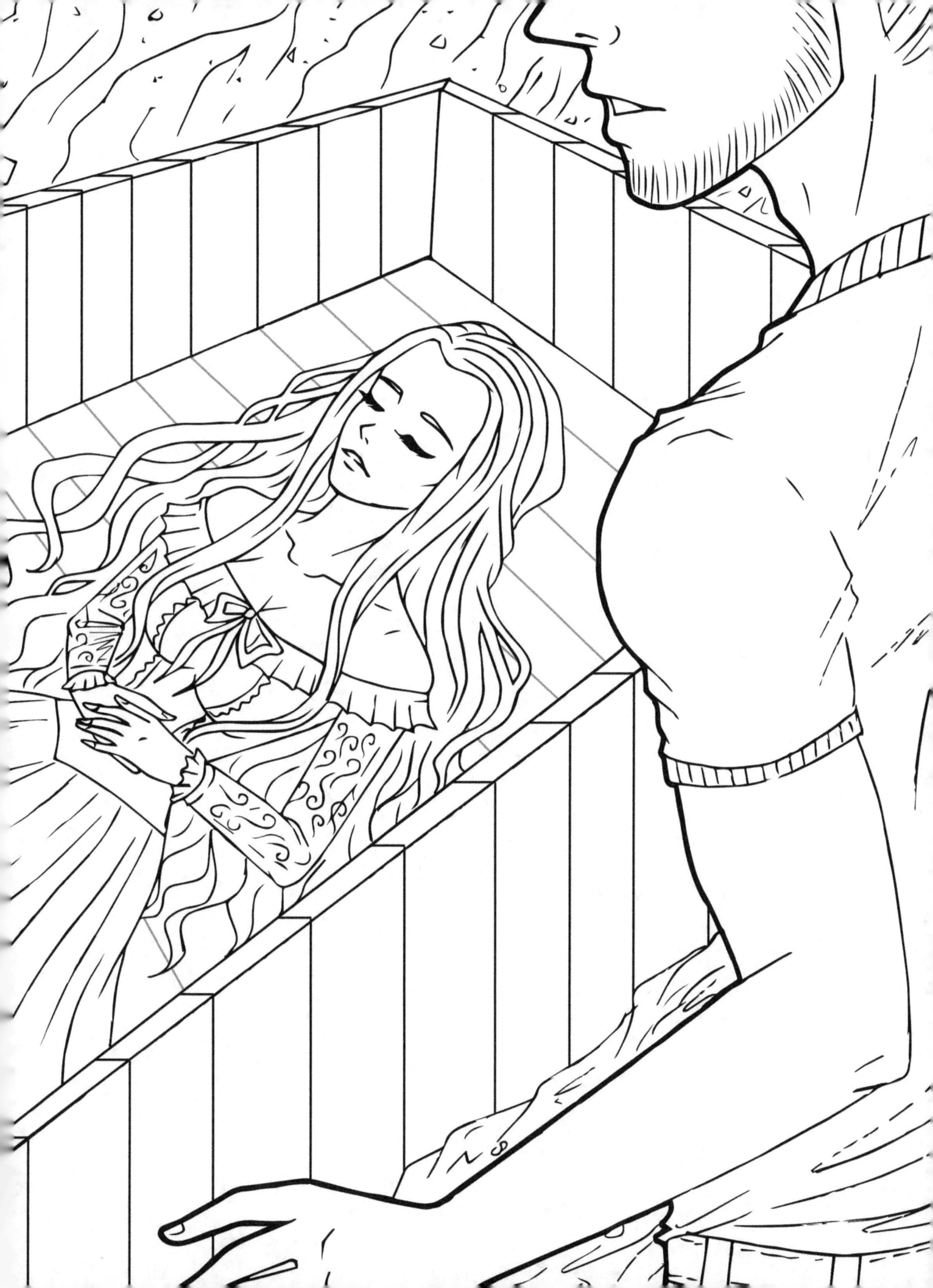

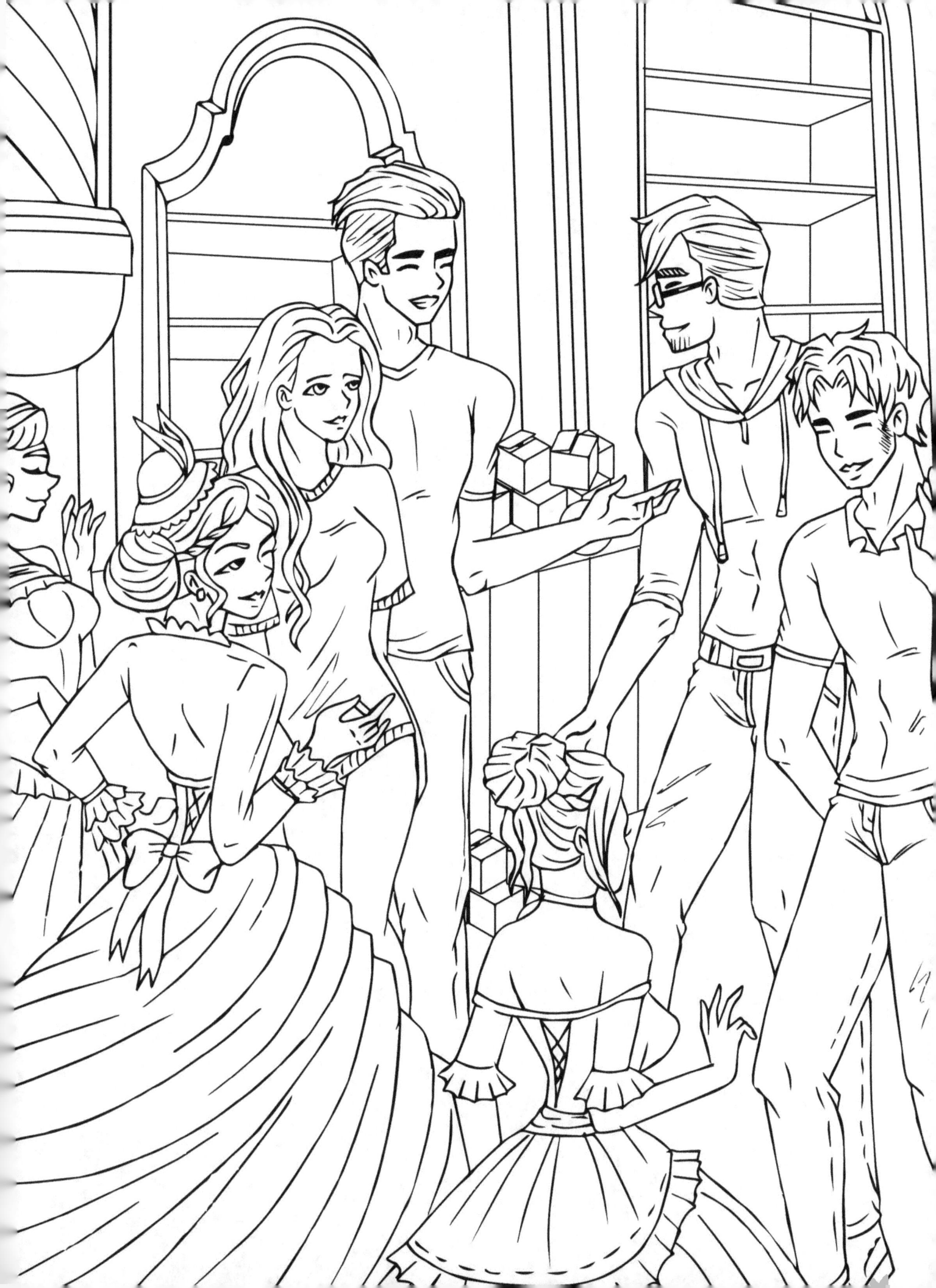

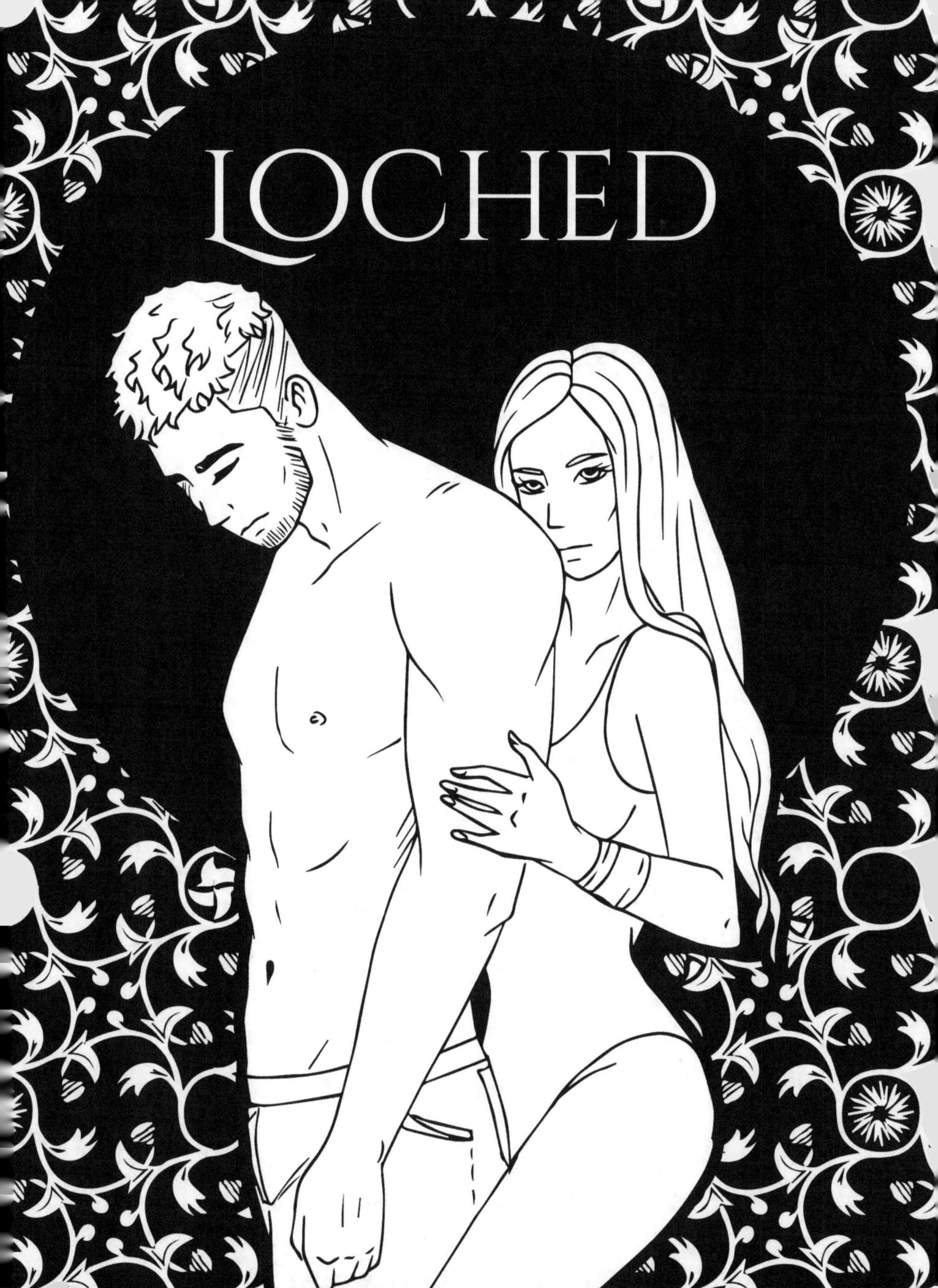

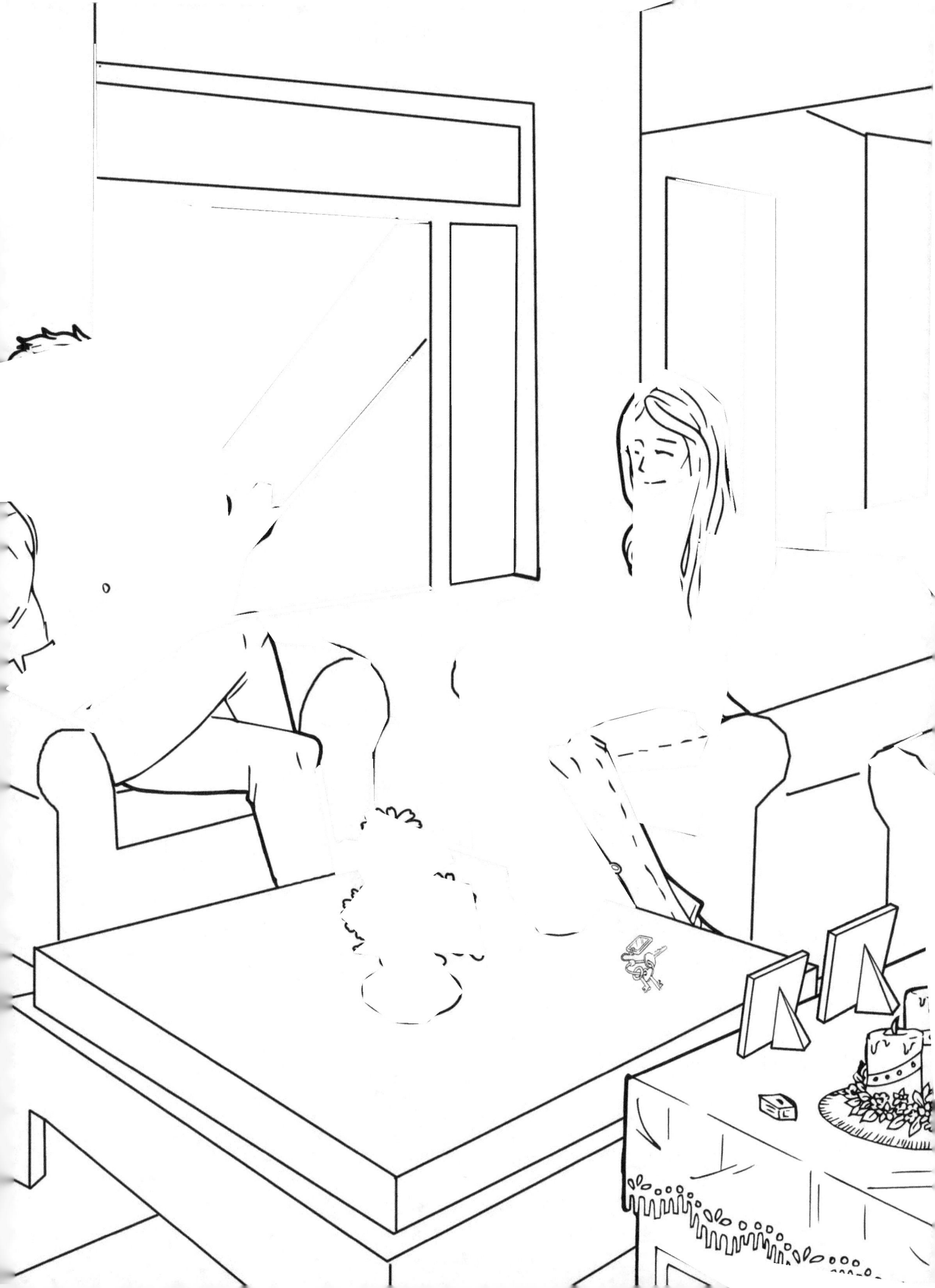

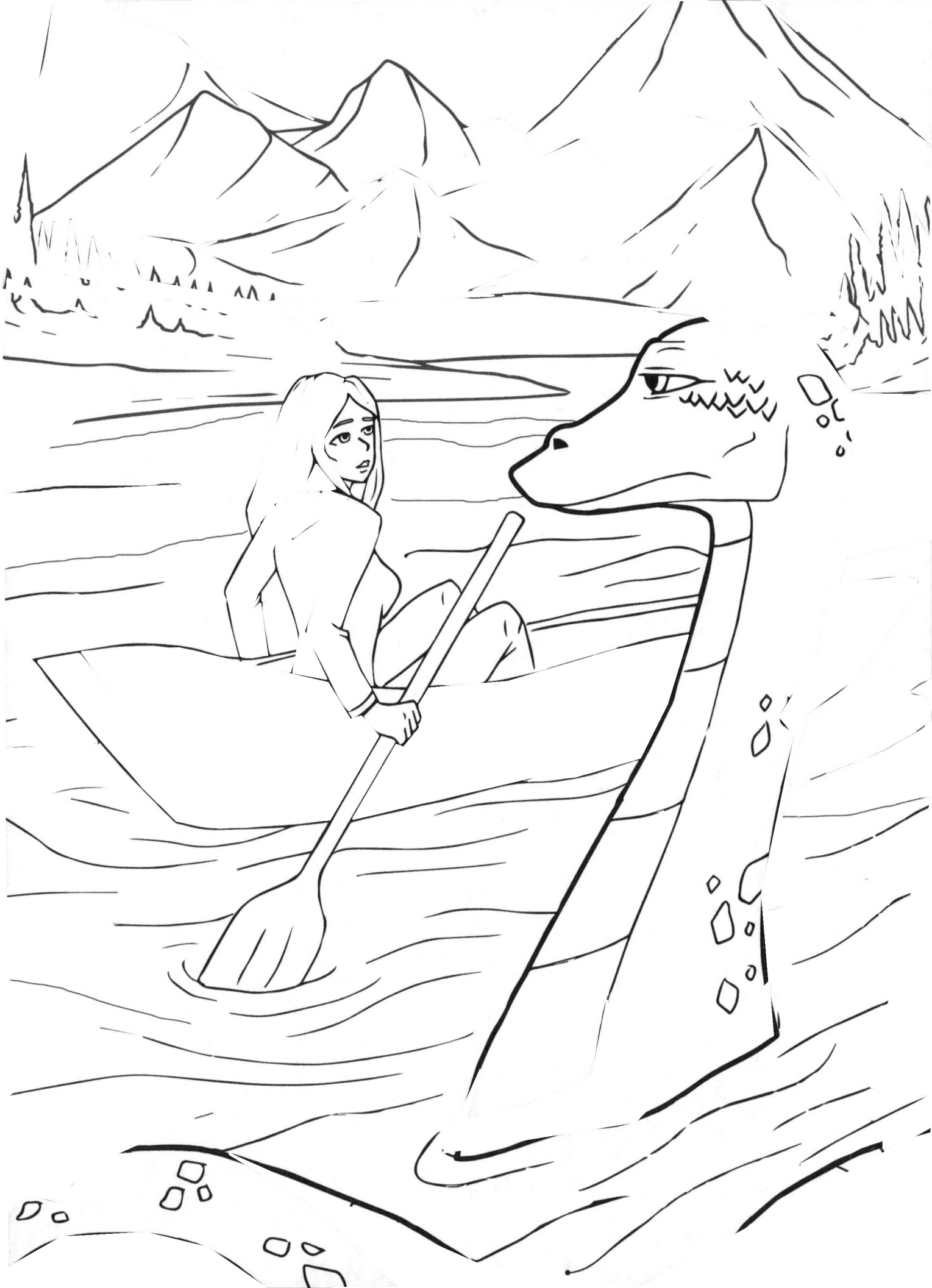

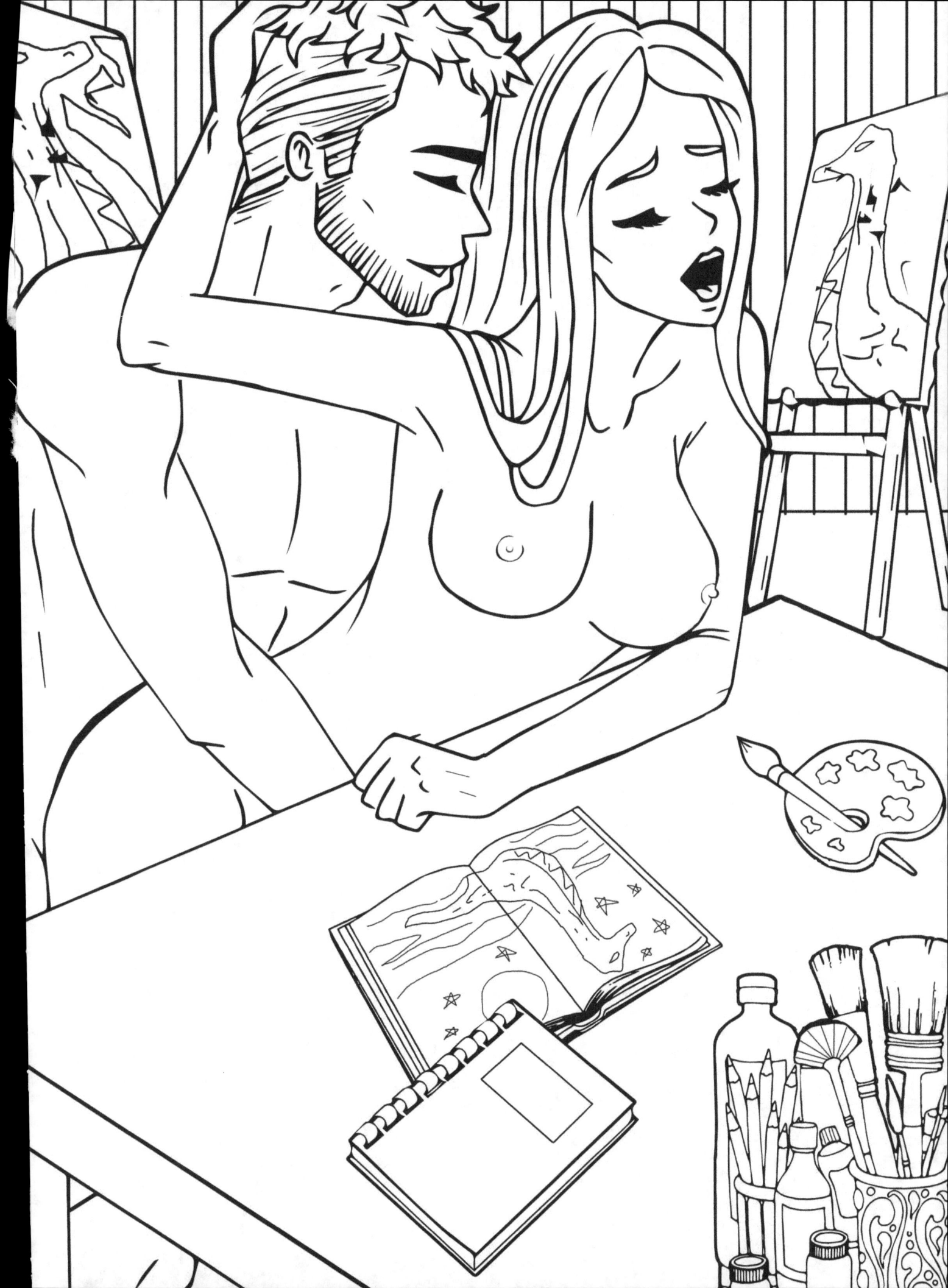

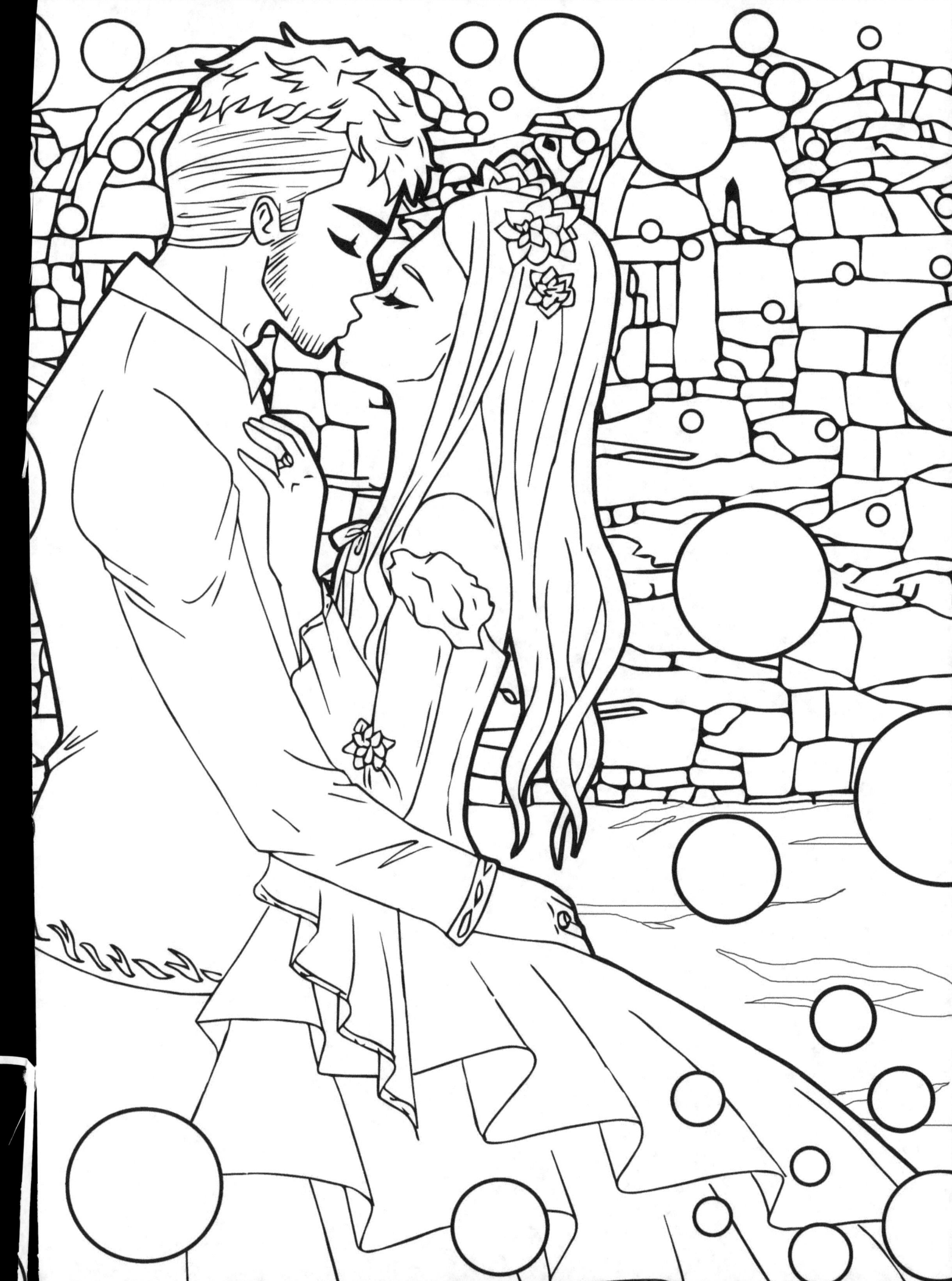

The Fury Family Series Coloring Book

© Gwyn McNamee 2022

SUPERNATURAL
LOVE STORIES
IN THE ABSURD